*EVERYTHING IS
NOT AS IT IS*

SINGULARITY
(interview)

Ilya Kogan

ISBN-13: 78-1718726499

ISBN-10: 171872649X

Russian text on page. 53
Русский текст на стр. 53

CONTENTS

1. OVERTURE

I really wanted to give interview about the singularity. However, there is a problem, there is no one wishing to interview me. However, there is a big desire. Then I remembered that Kissinger said that he hoped that in the room there are people who pose questions for prepared answers. He will answer these questions. After all questions are notoriously more than can be answered in the allotted time. That is, Kissinger pursued similar interviews.

I too have the answers and must write the questions. However, there are questions too. There is no journalist who will listen to me and will print interview in an article. Nevertheless, interview could be published in a booklet.

Case for a small, prepare a booklet with interview for publishing.

As usual, I write in Russian, to think only of the sense, not about choosing words. Then translate into English. This method helps me when tormented by insomnia. I mentally translate the English verses (usually Pushkin) or songs (usually Vertinsky). In severe cases, I put headphones and listen, walking through the apartment, bypassing bedroom, not to disturb my wife. I am listening to something like "Physics of the Impossible" by Michio Kaku, "The Age of Spiritual Machines", by Ray Kurzweil, or Old Greek Stories; it helps significantly.

Not to invent pseudonyms there are in work two individuals, conventionally the other doubled. The first interviewer name is "Question" or "Q". The second, named "Response" or "R".

Questions are grouped by themes, in agreement with Q and R.

At preparing to print interview there were made some changes and additions. This text is highlighted in italic.

2. INTRODUCTION

Q.   To the distinguished audience. I am honored to lead in this interview. The questions will answer Dr. of Technical Sciences Ilya Kogan. Dr. Kogan had authored more than 100 scientific publications, mostly in technical Diagnostics. Many of his publications were republished in English in the United States.

Did I correctly presented you?

R.   Yes, but I would add that Technical Diagnostics is a science, which is close to recognizing images. It can be argued that it relates to the field of computing and programming. However, in this cannot be ignored the analysis of the phenomenon, called singularity.

In my work, attention is drawn to the questions prior to the mathematics that is built over and come after the original thesis. This primarily relates to physics. As an example may serve publications in the field of quantum computers.

I have heard from very reputable scientists that there are sections where mathematics does not help to find out the crux of the problem. They said that there are cases when it is better to use for proof (in mathematics) reasoning, based on common sense. I would especially like to mention the outstanding mathematicians as I. M. Gelfand, A. Kolmogorov, M. Keldysh and V. Glushkov, from whom I heard such allegations.

Perhaps this was meant by Albert Einstein, expressing the proposal, which is mentioned in Micheo Kaku remarkable book "Physics of the impossible", «Einstein once said that unless a theory can be explained to a child, the theory was probably useless; that is, the essence of a theory has to be captured by a physical picture. So many physicists get lost in a thicket of mathematics that leads nowhere. However, like Newton before him, Einstein was obsessed by the physical picture; the mathematics would come later. For Newton, the physical picture was the falling apple and the moon. Were the forces that made an apple fall identical to the forces that guided the moon in its orbit? When Newton decided that the answer was yes, he created a mathematical architecture for the universe that suddenly unveiled the greatest secret of the heavens, the motion of celestial bodies themselves. »

Unfortunately, I have not been able to achieve neither discuss the original ideas that are the foundation of layers in the form of mathematical constructions.

Q.   How long have you interested in problems related to Singularity?

R.   Long before the notion of singularity was used in relation to computing. I have to analyze this concept (or this issue) in e.g. lectures of the usage of computers in research and design works. Popular were questions about whether the machine would think. In 1950, Stalin argued that the machine would never be a translator. I called a debate on the issue at the Institute. In fact, it was a discussion about the possible abilities of the machines. More about whether you can limit the possibilities of science. Discussion was banned by Party Secretary of the Institute; we cannot discuss the view of Stalin.

For example, my fortieth birthday (1969) was in Odessa beer café Gambrinus. We (the department staff) were sitting on small barrels (chairs) around a big barrel (table); one officer was reading his thoughts on the future of our Department. The Division will be called "Vysre on kurimo. This is reduction (sounding in Russian on the verge of decency) of "Computing systems on chicken brains". Author in several hours set forth justification for why I have chosen exactly chicken brains to create intellectual system (the concept of singularity was not yet widely known). An example is to emphasize that theme Singularity for me is not new. This is a topic I was interested in long before the described example. It was close to the Department work.

My journey to diagnosis (and science) in more detail is set out in the annex.

Q.   Please, do define concept of singularity.

R.   Under Singularity, I understand a system that has an IQ about an average human IQ. It is assuming that the system can pass the Turing test. For the computer system used in Jeopardy, was not measured IQ and, nevertheless, one could argue that it has passed the Turing test.

Q.   In the topic of singularity, it pays great attention to the human brain.

R.   It is natural because singularity is a program and a computer that is running this program. In singularity, you can divide software and "iron", but they are one entity. I would not "open America", e.g. R. Kurzweil rightly asserts that man is rather software, i.e. human personality can be described and stored as a file. The physical incarnation the singularity would define itself.

Q.   What do you say about the existence of consciousness in singularity?

R.   If a person is some software, then consciousness is some subprogram (a file) in it. If not, you will need to go beyond the laws of conservation. There, I am helpless. Similarly, you can talk about sex, about the mood and so forth.

Q.   Can there be a society, in which have equal rights to participate at the same time, people and computers, i.e. singularity.

R.   Certainly. The only condition is the proximity of the IQ of society members. This issue has already been discussed in my book SINGULARITY WHERE IS IT. (second edition), see on AMAZON. The first edition of the book was published in 2007.

Q.   The book's title says that you are putting in doubt the closeness of the emergence of the singularity.

R.   This is what I considered and tried to justify in the book.

Q.   Are you against the concept of singularity?

R.   Nothing of the kind! I am sure in its usefulness. I really like the description of singularity in brilliant R. Kurzweil's books. I am just not sure in the proximity of the occurrence of the singularity. My question is where it is. Now, April 2018 in the Congress is "judged" Facebook. It turned out that the "judges" showed their complete failure and a lack of understanding of the issues associated with the role, capabilities and performance of computing systems.

Nevertheless, it is already present and will be near future of our society, our country.

Q. Are you too severe?

R. On the contrary.

Q. Define your view of reality, for example, religion.

R. I am not religious. This is not only because I spent my life (up to 57 years) in a country where religion was referred to as "the opium of the people". I long ago realized that many public philosophies are equivalent to religion; that the most Orthodox religion is historical materialism. Especially its practice. After all, the Communists raised possibility of establishing socialism with a human face. I long ago realized that many religions are Orthodox political parties.

The basis of my worldview lies in the inviolability of the CONSERVATION LAWS. It is from these laws follows the impossibility of instant actions. They do not allow infinite speeds. They require the relativity of observation of the phenomena of nature. The phenomena taken by A. Einstein for the name of his theory. They do not allow the creation of something from nothing. That is, the universe (space, time, energy) is eternal and infinite. Of them, follow the behavior of the gyroscope and the first law of Newton.

I would emphasize that this does not diminish the greatness of the scientists who had formulated those for the first time.

Of these, followed statements as:

- Anything that is not forbidden is mandatory! (T. H. White).

- Evolution is not evil-minded; it is inevitable (A. Einstein).

Then there came for sure, there would be people, and singularity.

3. THE SETTING UP
OF SINGULARITY

Q.   Stay more on your vision of the singularity.

R.   Singularity is a powerful software system. For work, singularity requires a powerful computing system.

- Such a system needs a large memory for its storage and work.

- It requires significant computational performance from machine on which the program would work.

- It requires high system reliability.

Q.   It seem you have said that everything is already there.

Ilya Kogan

R.   The system that, in my opinion, passed the Turing test has been demonstrated in the game of Jeopardy. However, it was only an experiment that demonstrated the principal possibility. I play chess, but between Kasparov and me is a huge distance. Here are years of labor and much more.

Q.   Transcribe what else. As you said "much more".

R.   There are many problems.

1. Philosophical problems, such as

- The place of singularity in the society.

- Coexistence of singularity and human.

- Would the singularity be represented as a single instance, or this would be a set of separate systems.

- The duration of life of the singularity.

- Place of the singularity in the evolution of nature.

2. Technical problems.

- Development of system requirements for hardware, which will operating the singularity.

- Creation of a computing system that will provide sustainable and reliable operation of the singularity.

- Singularity coexistence with the environment.

- Possible technical limitations and their causes.

3. Mathematical software systems (Singularity).

- Creation of algorithms for singularity.

Issues listed were not isolated and their solutions affect each other. Each item requires serious consideration.

Q.   Let us stop on the technical problems.

R.   There are opinions that computing power that can be created in the universe reaches 10^{80} os (operation per second). Theoretical calculation is correct, but it is not considered survivability of the system and service requirements. It may be that computing power will be much lower than projected, and even lower than the required for the work of the singularity.

Ensuring reliable functioning requires the introduction of additional equipment, which will reduce performance and increase the system volume. Redundancy increases the size and reduces system performance. Redundancy introduces into the system structure additional parts, which impossible to test when are used only working system inputs.

I understand that "may be" is not an evidence, but the issue should be considered.

Q. What difficulties or contradictions of a technical nature you can name.

R. Just a few examples

- Speed of work. If true is the principle of doubling capacity / performance in two years (or even one hundred years), for a hundred million years, the speed of the technical base would grow to enormous magnitude. The value of 10^{80} os would seem miserable. However, instant appearance of the experimental results allows infinite speeds.

- Increased speed requires an increase in the density of the elements and reduce their size, as a result, would increase sensitivity to external fields. This makes to fall survivability of the singularity.

- There is a problem of introduction of redundancy this can stop the speed increase.

Of course, if allowed infinite speed, then all the problems addressed in the present work, are disappearing. Let me remind that I am a supporter of conservation laws, and not of divine magic. I presume the existence of a powerful (very powerful) God, however not almighty with no limit.

Q.   Let us move to software.

R.   There are only assumptions about such systems. The only example is the human brain. There has been done some suggestions how the brain organizes thinking which are not flawless.

For example, there is known a phenomenon of learning. To a man are given the rules of some game unfamiliar to him. After listening, he immediately begins to play this game and even beats his teacher. It is hard to explain this phenomenon based on neural networks, genetic algorithms, or recursive calculations. It is difficult to build the desired path of evolution in small steps on these principles.

Experiments with structures like finite state machines allow to argue that this could achieved by evolution in small steps. There is needed software that enables you to create (or simulate) a structure similar to a finite state machine and change this structure in the process of information exchange with the environment.

Q.　What are the differences in the evolution of singularity and living creatures?

R.　The evolution of singularity is fundamentally different from the evolution of living beings. The brain can change its structure in small increments from generation to generation. The new generation of singularity can be significantly different from the previous one. For this should be included possibilities in mathematical and technical support. These capabilities are developed by known methods, technical specifications, and technical project. Further is prototyping and experimentation.

Q.　How are mathematical and technical design connected?

R.　For example, ensuring reliability is possible affecting the quality of the element base. On the other hand, you can build reliable structures from unreliable elements. You can conduct testing and repair in real-time. You can improve by secure coding. You can build a system of reliable computations. An example is the comparison of recalculation results. All of these methods allow combining.

Q.　Let us proceed to philosophy.

R.   Here, I am afraid to express my opinion. After all, this will be handled by much more intelligent "creature" - singularity. Of cause, if such a system is possible. I.e. the evolution already has created the most powerful possible intellectual system - the human brain.

If the singularity may have intelligence, much larger than human intelligence, the human has no place in the future society. Remember, in the "Planet of the apes" people are in cages in a Zoo.

Q.   Your opinion on the existence of singularity.

R.   In the universe inevitable would appear singularity. It takes roughly five billion years.

If the universe is closed, then the lifetime of singularity is about 10 billion years. Let me remind that this happens in the context of the law of accelerating development. I am a believer in this law. In a new cycle of development of the universe, everything repeats.

If the universe is not closed, it will grow indefinitely. Accordingly increases the lifetime and development of singularity. However, fundamental changes in the development of the singularity must occur in the first few billion years after its groundwork.

Ilya Kogan

It is assumed that at this initial period of existence would be resolved all philosophical questions.

If the space is infinite then there are local universes. However, there would no principal differences.

Singularity could not be able to move from one local universe to another. It would be destroyed by the radiation of the Big Bang in neighboring universes when it would moving in the space between universes. This happens for an open local universe as well.

Migrating the rudiments of life between local universes, the radiation of Big Bang explosions would not hurt.

Q. The above is a fantasy, or it may have a scientific basis?

R. Many is written in my books (see references in "RESULTS" 2017 on AMAZON). Sometimes in the form of semi - fiction, as the results of Professor Multyrock in its Theory of Absolute Space.

However, the described "Laboratory of Analysis of Development" (LAD) may have a scientific background, based on the theory of evolution. Today LAD can start creating an experimental base on 3D printers.

Apparently when addressing issues of thinking in the wildlife, you must allocate the plots of the nervous system, which are similar to the type like structure of the finite state machines.

It is obvious that for human it will be neocortex. What plots are for dolphins or octopus? What it is for a dog, which is drawing a car? This can be determined without destructive experiments.

Not all experiments today feasible. Experiments study the theories of absolute Space is not available today, but are possible in principle.

Socio - political issues

Q.   What is the future of humanity?

R.   Thanks to the genius of E. Teller practically disappeared the danger of humanity self-destruction. Thermonuclear weapons made the war meaningless. All sorts of "human rights defenders" (or rather the fire raiser) even invented (for E. Teller) an Award (Ig Nobel Prize). However, they only made greater the genius of E. Teller.

I wrote about this on many occasions. There are two types of future society.

- Mixed (humans and machines) society.

- Pure machine society.

Q.   Is a transition process from today into the "light" of the future?

R.   Apparently, it is going to be something close to that described in my books. On Earth will be one State with one language. The population of the order of one to two billion. Population will live in cities – houses surrounded by zones like Orlando. The main provision, defining life will be "code of stability." Each House will have up to a million residents. Apartment walls will be covered with wallpaper - television screens. On these screens in addition to current programs will be possible to see (to call) any cultural or historic event in the desired language.

The political structure is close to the United States. Group of homes are combined in States that have a central Government. Under the ceiling screen is a tape, which allows see polls, referendums and voting. This allows quickly determine the view of society and makes unnecessary crowded protests in the street.

Q.   What is the contribution to civilization by countries?

R.   I am not competent, but one case I will tell. In the Cathedral of Notre Dame, a guide is not talking to us about the Cathedral but on the contribution of France to democracy. She requested us to say our opinion. I said I know that France (democracy) gave the world the guillotine, and England (monarchy) gave the Hyde Park. In her view, I realized that she regrets that she has no guillotine.

Q.   What about Russia?

R.   Russia is well worthy for a place in the second ten developed countries. Indeed, in the world there are United States, China, France, Britain, and so on. Every politician in Russia who foretells that Russia, known to be the first place in the world objectively is the worst enemy of Russia. Every politician who constantly does not compare Russia with Norway is an enemy of Russia.

Q.   What holds back the development of civilization?

R.   Political Correctness. It is hard to find anything more harmful to the society. Even the introduction of the sport to Afro-American lesser influence on society. It is just hidden racism.

Q.   Would it be possible to fight the huge disproportions in developed and poorest countries in the world, and the gap between the different segments of the population within countries?

R.   Today, technologically it is possible to produce enough food and basic life support products that will be available (practically free) to the entire population of the Earth.

Difficulty, that is more substantial, is in destroying psychological barriers. For example, "Why for Trump, Gates it is available, and for me not." How to destroy animal envy of gratified, dressed persons living in a comfortable apartments, to the richer ones - I do not know. However, I am sure that this is possible.

EPILOGUE

Q.   Your vision of the future.

R   I do not know, however...

As I already wrote, humanity will reach the general welfare. It is closer than the nearest singularity. Everybody can be provided with meals, apartment, and entertainment. Everything is made by machines. There is no diseases.

However, desire and envy are irretrievable. For example, a million of persons want the most luxurious Palace atop the Mount Elbrus. Of course, everyone needs but there is one vertex. Who would decide whom to give it? Apparently, without Instructor of Communist Party District, as under socialism, the society could not survive.

Moreover, here the singularity appeared. Here deliberately to each according to the needs. What are ones needs? S. Lem did not write about life of the singularity, the Solaris Ocean.

Apparently, you can only write about it for today's humanity. I tried touching this subject in my brochure, which I called
"EVERYTHING IS NOT AS IT IS".

Conclusion

Q.   In conclusion, let me thank Dr. Kogan for his work.

R. I would like to express thanks to the audience for the patience.

4. LIFE (APPENDIX)

Use this chapter as a memory note for professors and lawyers of the "free world". Using new speech of Big Brother, they called themselves Democrats.

The clintons or sanderses are well aware for what benefits, wealth and power they are struggling.

4.1. Everything is simple

Thinking about my life I remember my mom, she came from the military office (1945), where to her was presented a paper about the death of David (my brother).

Suddenly, I heard a terrible groan, cry, or howl. She sang, "In vain the old lady is waiting for her

son back home, she would told, she would wept ...”
She brought the axe above her head, which I had a
chance to withdraw. Yes, at 50 she became an old,
very old, woman. Very old, very old, she hunched
and her face become wan and drawn in a few
minutes. This scene and a terrible sound periodically
do visiting me. Apparently, this would be the last
image in my life.

For every mother her son is endlessly dear. The
Commander can send millions into the fire (Rzhev) or
into the waters of Volga; maybe one out of a hundred
will reach Stalingrad. Then he calmly say as Zhukov
did, “Women give birth to new”.

I looked back and found a huge gap between
my childhood and today. For this reason, my life is
briefly described and highlighted in critical (or funny)
points. The reader can be surprised by dates. In the
United States, much was decades before. However,
the production of modern weapons in the USSR did
not yield in quality and surpassed in quantity. This is
not interested in the United States to Socialists, which
are called Democrats. They will remember the Galich
songs when would be in Gulag, of established
country. God forbid!

I recall a few episodes of life, which could
significantly influence it.

1941, I went to buy food, returned, and our train left. I sat down on the one, which, as was told to me, is going in the right direction. Platform with glasses for shells. Came a group of boys. First, they eat everything I bought. Then play cards and the two winners said that they would take my hands and feet and throw from the train. I opened the penknife, took in the second hand a shell, and said, do come. The leader liked it. He was noticeably larger than the rest.

He said that I could recoup what I did. The gang galloped to Uzbekistan for the winter, where they "come across" and were determined to an orphanage. In the spring they stick up the orphanage and rode back to steal in Siberia. In Uzbekistan to steal was dangerous. Uzbeks scored with boots to death.

I did not have to participate in their affairs; I played as a couple with the leader. We won and others hated me.

When in the spring were sold the stolen goods at a Bazaar, I saw my mom. Tracked and went to see her. She sold something from things and in that evening should go from Magellan to Andijan where in a village lived (found via Buguruslan) Middle brother. He left Echelon three weeks before me. I explained to her the situation and said that necessarily will come.

In the evening, at the station Gorchakovo was a roundup. Our leader was seized as a deserter. All ran away, and I found mom in her train.

Brother soon was called to the army. We moved under Fergana, where lived the wife of mom's brother. It turned out that to school I could not go, on the way boys beat me because I was a "dirty kirk". I could not go to class with a face filled with blood. I went as a machine operator apprentice to a textile complex. Work was a week from 7 am to 7 pm, followed by 7 pm to 7 am. Without weekends and 30 min break for food (which I have not).

1944, was freed Nikolayev, and we went back. I entered the plant as operator. Then in the industrial school as the Modeler on wood and in evening school. Brother was killed at January 21, 1945 and in his last letter, he asked me to learn.

1947, passed the last school exams, and according to results should get a gold medal. I was given all documents as for gold medal, but no certificate. It came the end of entering exams, and I cannot apply. I was called to school Director and he prompts to select for what subjects I do put four and he would give me a simple certificate. Come to the Institute of Communication and was accepted without examination.

Ilya Kogan

1950, finishing third year and mother had a stroke, she was paralyzed (the left side of the body). First, she was in the hospital and then at home.

In the morning, I go to the hospital and from there to the Yacht Club. Eat stale bread and water. I was given a boat at a student station. I noticed on the bank an accustomed boy and came to call him into the boat. He said that would introduce me to girls. I meet, and one with a charming smile agree to go into the boat. Since that time, we are inseparable about 70 years.

Arranged with a woman who will live and help my mother. In October, I got a telegram to come urgently, mother left one. Doors were open, jump into the apartment and hear a desperate cry, rather quick, give podsov (thing that helps paralyzed). Go to pour podsov into the toilet, which was at the end of the yard. I come back and discover that in the cold apartment, in addition to the bed, in which is mom, a broken stool and a table, there was nothing. There were no rags or paper, only mountains of garbage on the floor. Two small basement rooms, without electric lighting, the nearest water in the yard around the corner. In grocery stores, shelves were empty (1950), but no money anyway.

Established life, get up before light and start fire in the stove, feed Mommy and sit down for the tutorials. In the evening, go to Mila. Now, half a century after, I realized that she was my rescue, I was not thinking about the future. Endless, dark, winter evenings; what terrifying thoughts could be born in my head.

1951, It was discovered that for months I had not been at the lectures. I came for a day, passed the exams, laboratory, control works, tests and so on. Rumor were that sick Mommy is my invention, in Nikolayev I was because of a girl.

I was called to a meeting of the Bureau of the Komsomol organization. Question was about my exclusion and as a consequence the army.

My friend says to the Secretary of the Party Committee of the Institute Panshin (he was Chairman of the collection Commission and contributed to my University entrance), which was present, that is needed a break. He tells the truth, and Panshin asks me because in two months I must go to internship in Chisinau. I invented that the doctors said that in a month my mother rises.

They begin to offer help. Showing my student book where only fives I told that would manage myself. One girl said that she could travel to Nikolayev and help. I blew up and roared; thou you shalt serve mom podsov and sleep with me on the table. ... The silence and the meeting was closed.

A month later, I once again arrive in Odessa, and there was a telegram awaits me on the death of my mother. Funeral, I left an open apartment and straight from the cemetery went to Odessa. Started a normal student life.

In postgraduate school, I have not been left, but the appointment was very successful. In Yerevan, was built an underground radio station, where I worked as a fitter and setter with the best specialists of the country.

1953, arrive in Nikolayev for Mila, we married.

However, her "friends" warned me.

- You lived a hard life. Nobody knew the truth. No one I invited home, newer I told anyone about my life at that time.

- She is a horridly pampered kitten; was called Aristocrat at the University.

- You will not find a common language; consider this.

Reckless youth. In five days, Mila worked with me, we were given an excellent apartment (half of a house with a big yard). She has a very strong coloratura soprano. Voice resounded far into the mountains, and I knew all the operas and operettas parties. I listen, in the evenings, to her concerts in the Gorge near a river.

Many years have passed, and we all this time are inseparable. It seems that we increasingly gravitate to each other. Of course, time affects. I have a constant weight, but a bit bald. It seems I am now not so firmly stand on two feet on the floor as on one hand on the railing of the balcony at that time. Mila retained mobility and so on.

1956, father-in-law calls us to Nikolayev. April 16 was abolished serfdom; we have the right to leave our jobs. However, in Nikolayev for me was no work, as well as in other 63 cities where I wrote. I worked temporarily as a Carpenter. I went to Moscow and in ministries' corridors asked each solid man. Therefore, I met the Deputy Director of the Kirovakan "NIIAvtomatika".

We prepared to go, but I was called for four months on retraining officer courses. During this time came refusal from Kirovakan. Father in law went with me to the Second Secretary of the Regional CP Committee, and he helped me get position as an engineer at radio Center. A month later, I was fired. I have been looking at dirt road for a rocky plot to kill myself.

We took a counsel and decided that I should go to Kirovakan, and say that I was in the camps and the letter did not receive. Arrived, I immediately given a position and an excellent apartment. The letter was not from the management.

Job put me to a gold mine "Technical Diagnostics".

1986, we in United States, from 70 (1999) in retirement.

4.2. From the other side

I, Ilya Veniaminovich Kogan, *Jew by nationality*, was born September 5, 1929 in the town Voznesensk. The structure of the first phrase was dictated as obligatory, by Colonel, Member of the CPSU, and head of Odessa Voroshilovsky District Military Committee. In 1952, the year we wrote our autobiographies for the award of officer rank. Words in italic were removed by the order of the head of Kotayk District Military Committee of Armenia in the 1953. Odessa's biography he gave me, saying that it is a document, certified by signature and the seal of Voroshilovsky military Committee. It could be valuable in future.

In 1932, a flood destroyed the town of Voznesensk and our House. We moved to Mykolaiv, where rented a kitchen in a basement. Most of it was occupied by a huge Russian oven. Oven required lots of fuel and in winter, it was cold. There were no electricity (in our kitchen), no sewage, and water supply. In my surrounding, there were a lot like me. We were missing near everything, but we were not starving. Note that even the Holodomor not concerned cities. Communists strangled the countryside population; access to cities was closed by the army.

1934, I and the other children ran out to the street. Clapped and sang when was flying a plane or a big car rides. Family photos can be counted on the fingers of one hand.

There were in my life bright sides too. In our yard lived: Dina Yakovlevna Zaslavskaya, her children were in the USA. Historian Vladimir Vyacheslavovich with wife - aunt Dusya. Engineer Anton Yakovlevich Karno with wife – a Doctor Sofiya Solomonovnovna. I was the only child.

In Nikolayev lived my aunt, they have had no children. Her husband uncle Seryozha presented me splendid designers and different sets of tools. He presented wonderful books, subscribed for newspapers, and different publication like "For skillful hands".

1937, A.Y. bought a receiver and camera. Thru the gate of a military base that was next to us entered tanks and cannons. State delivered (free) a radio spiker. At the corners on the posts, the state put up loudspeakers.

It was an unpleasant duty, getting around the streets and collect horse and cow dung. From it with coal crumb, we sculpted cakes, which were used as fuel in winter.

Yet, something was better than for many of my peers. Garden, in spring surrounded by multicolored lilac and other flowering bushes and trees. Three enormous silk tree giving food for two months. In addition, an elm, tremendous tree with divergent three trunks, branches were flexible as ropes, with a huge thick crown.

There were our tents, Indian outfits and bows. There I fixed my 10-year-old brother, by ropes. Closed windows and the door. I did a chess move and went to tell him. First, I tested how he is bounded. I lost and perplexed, how he manages so quickly come look the position and again climb, and bind. That he can play "blindly" I did not believe.

My brother I adored, he was one of the best fighters, the teenage city champion in chess and swimming. The coach of the street football team. I have learned, being in kinder garden, along with my brother the first four classes.

1939, bread was rationed.

In 1941, the war started. We evacuated. First my brother, and then I missed the train. I flecked with some sort of a gang of thieves. Then I lived in an orphanage. I met mom in Margilan in 1942. Moved with her to brother in a village near Andijan. He was soon called to the army.

We moved into the textile town near Fergana. We lived in a room together with an elderly woman and mother with a daughter. They have survived the blockade. Only two, from a big family, survived. From them I know the details of the Leningrad blockade.

To the school I could not walk. In the street, I was stopped by boys who enjoyed clobber "zhidenka" (a Jew boy). If I tried to fight back, they grabbed my hands and beaten until the face has been bathed in blood. I used to run home and cry, not from pain, but from unfair insults.

Went to work as machine operator apprentice. The work was without weekends; a week from 7 am to 7 pm, a week from 7 pm to 7 am, 30 minutes break for food, which almost never was. At that time, I dreamt, in my dreams day and night only food (any food). The feet were swollen from hunger and malaria attack every other day.

1943, my new router has its own electric engine. All other machines were moving from the pulley at axle under the ceiling.

In 1944 returned to Mykolaiv. I worked at a factory. Without shoes, I was not allowed to enter the plant barefooted. In the wooden white pads, I was ashamed and I walked to evening school barefooted. Brother wrote that I must went to school, but instead of his officer's certificate came a death certificate and his orders. I went to trade school and to an evening school. Went according to my age in the eighth grade (5, 6, and 7 I have not attended).

After ending school (1947), the officials tried to disrupt my admission in the Institute. According to the results, I was deserved a gold medal, but was given a simple certificate with a big delay. It was already too late to take the entrance exams, but I was accepted.

Moreover, here I am in the student dormitory. I sleep on sheets as other 17 my roommates. For the first time in my life, comfortable, fun, friendly.

It was difficult, I need to work and help my mother. Suddenly she had a stroke. She may not be alone paralyzed in a cold and dark basement. I look for her in Nikolayev and "learn" in Odessa. The second stroke and I am alone.

However, I finally felt all the charm of student life

1950, participate in the creation of an amateur TV station. In our room, one student (of 18) has a camera.

1952, assembler and adjuster of a powerful underground radio station. In addition to generators with lamps as my height, there are many interesting things. For example, the regenerators of the atmosphere and hermetic protection. I have my own camera.

In 1956, the father-in-law convinced us to move to Nikolayev. It turned out that I could find only temporally work as Carpenter. I was highly qualified in installation and configuration of electronic equipment. It was one of the most sought-after profession in the USSR at that time. However, this was the policy of the members of the Communist Party of the Soviet Union. I wrote to 63 regional centers, but nowhere was I needed. We returned to Armenia.

1957 simulate the control systems on analog computers. Programming on digital machines (1960).

I was three times invited by famous professors in postgraduate school. For various formal purposes, I was not allowed to entrance exams.

Now in the United States (2016) was Election Company. Professors and students want to move the country into socialism. It is hard not to believe the lies of the Socialists. Churchill said that one who does not believe in socialism in 18 has no heart, but if one believe in 30, one has no brains.

1987 simulate neural networks and genetic algorithms in the United States. Appears Internet.

This is my life, but this is the reality created by the members of the Communist Party of the Soviet Union. This is what is called for by professors and students in the USA. Apparently, "they do not know what they do". If, God allowed and they win, they would be the first martyred to the Gulag they created.

I lived with socialism for 57 years. I had to meet and had lengthy conversations with very high positioned people. I studied the information flows in a typical Region for National automated control system. I was a scientific supervisor of this project.

My first job was in 1942, Assistant of an electric assembler. In fact, I worked from early childhood. The cleaning, furnace and so on. After the Institute, I was sent to the construction of a powerful underground radio facility in the mountains of Armenia.

Without supervisors defended Ph.D. and Doctor of Science dissertations. Next morning the academician Glushkov said: what have you done with my Cyber Center. It buzzes like a disturbed hive. Kogan from aside got 15:0.

Lived and worked in Yerevan, Kirovakan, Nikolayev, Odessa and Riga.

In 1986 moved to New York, United States. In the United States worked with my wife to 70, and here we are pensioners. We live on the third floor of own house. Below are children and grandchildren who do not have time to visit us. They speak to me only in Russian; English is forgettable.

We are living together (married in 1953) and friends "go away". Those that are, do not drive and do not go down the stairs; we talk on the phone and occasionally visit them. We try to be mobile and yet it manages to; lifts-chair on stairs yet is not required.

2000, pensioner, many computers, photo cameras, car, refrigerators, TV, RADIO-phones. Automatically is maintained temperature. In the street, passers-by have phones-computers. Rarely an important event happen that someone was not captured it on video.

Traveled a lot; in Europe, for example, were more than dozen times. Were in Japan, Singapore, Argentina, Brazil, and so on.

Was fond of gymnastics and rowing. In 1952 at the all-Union competition, was the second. Spectators at the Bank argued that our kayak first crossed the finish line. To me (secretly) was told that judges could not give first place to not a party member and a Jew. The champion in a month would go to the World Championships, abroad. Saying that the second became champion there.

List of my qualifications, only those that have been confirmed officially.

1942, Assembler of telephone networks (4-th level).
1943, Miller (5-th level).
1944, Toolmaker (6-th level).
1945, Molder (4-th level).
1945, Caster (4-th level).
1945, Carpenter (4-th level).
1946, Carpenter (red wood) (5-th level).
1947, Modeler (6-th level).
1952, Radio technician Engineer (diploma with honors).
1964, have defended the dissertation on the scientific degree of Candidate of Technical Sciences (Ph.D.). Moscow, USSR ACADEMY of SCIENCES Institute of Automation (the result of the vote, 16 for and 1 against).
1978, have defended the dissertation on the scientific degree of the Doctor of Technical Sciences. Kiev, Institute of Cybernetics of AS of Ukraine (vote 15 for, 0 against).

How things have changed for my life.

A LITTLE BIT OF POLITICS

I grew up as an ordinary Soviet boy. Talented "engineers of human souls" mihalkovs and marshaks inserted all in my head. I grew up as a convinced atheist. I was convinced that bourgeois want to take away my "happy childhood". Believed that religion is the opium of the people. Did not understand that the most Orthodox religion is teaching of the CPSU members. That many religions are political parties.

1933 Our worst enemies are capitalists. No more awful then Kolchak, Denikin and the like can be. Lenin defended the King only playing chess.

At the same time, I repeated with the Rabbi doleful prayer for my father and talked a lot with the Rabbi. Uncle Volodya discussed with me stories from ancient Egypt to the present day. A lot he talked about occurrence of religions and about "enemies of the people" like Trotsky. Women, which I saved in the evenings from mosquito with smoke, reminded me that I should study hard. Otherwise, I would not get the percentage.

In the year 1936 at the huge square "61 Communards", was an open process at the grandly people. There was sued a gang "speculators and blood drinkers". Apparently, by chance, there were only Jews. However, in the crowd was told that finally is given to Jews good punishment. A member of this gang was mother's elder sister Hawa. She lived with her daughter and son in a little dark room, where except rags, an old bed, one bedside table and a stool, was nothing. Later I learned that such processes took place in other cities. That is, it was a purposeful action of members of the CPSU throughout the country.

About the origin of the name of the square said a plate about these Communards, shot in the square. Uncle Volodya said that these were bandits and thieves, captured during raids in bazaars. They were caught and shot not in one day and in different places.

1939 Nazi Germany and its leaders, friends and enemies at the same time. Many teenagers had the swastika on their hands.

I do not know what instinct warned me from telling this in kindergarten and then to teachers at school. For the first time in 1939 A.Y., looking at my reviewing mountain of old books and negatives (photo of all "enemies of the people"), said that I should not tell anyone about this. Otherwise, uncle Volodya and he would be arrest. However, you for what, I asked, after all, this junk is from his attic. Because I was not told, was the reply. With A.Y. I photographed, exhibited and published photo. With him discussed the fantastic machines that I assembled by designers, presented by Uncle Serezha.

I did not realize that I say one thing, think another, and do some third. Through the years, I have noticed that this is done by majority. Apparently, the Homo Sovieticus had innate (reflex) since ancient times. Why else they searched for Rurik.

2000, about Kolchak, Denikin and others are created movies and they with honor reburied in Russia.

I was asked many times whether I, a citizen of United States, have the right to discuss Russia's problems. I will not dwell on the issue of freedom of expression.

I worked in Russia for more than 40 years (for pension is enough 25). My rationalization proposals and research have given multimillions for economic. Both of my older brothers were officers and killed at the front. My mother had two brothers. Moses, full Cavalier of the St. George Cross, was killed at the front in 1943. Victor, he commanded of artillery of Stalingrad (according to published memoirs) and retired as first Deputy Commander of the Kiev military district.

I was expelled by "Patriots - anti-Semites".

They have no right to speak about Russia. However, they again decide.

MY WAY INTO DIAGNOSTICS

In 1952, in the P/B 1 of Yerevan I first encountered with testing of logical devices. Security and order of work of equipment provided by complex relay circuits. They contain hundreds of open relay contacts, which have not work properly. Finding a faulty contact anticipated visually. I built for this test system.

In 1959, the Institute received a digital computer. Machine start working, but my first program did not run. In an accompanying documentation was written in bold: **"The manufacturer guarantees proper operation of the machine with the right tests running"**. However, one shift operation was carried out incorrectly, even though in the test were eleven operations for checking it. The analysis showed that two operations is enough and test would be good for checking shift.

Then I developed a "complete theory for test building", which was criticized (completely) by Ter-Mikayelyan. However, he recommended me to A.

Lyapunov at the Institute of Applied Mathematics of the USSR ACADEMY of SCIENCES.

In the year 1962 at the international symposium in Moscow, my report "Control of Logical Devices" was listened in English (simultaneous interpretation), by Professor J. P. Roth, who in 1964 proposed algorithm for designing test sets (D-Cubs). Proceedings of the Symposium with my report were published in the United States in English. It is hard to imagine that J. P. Roth had no copy of this book. Our reports were in the same volume. This was prior to the filing of his first work on diagnostics for publishing, but references to my work he did not placed. Report of J. P. Roth at the symposium was not on the diagnostics ("Pragmatic Theory of Algorithms"). My first publication (1958) he hardly have seen, but he knew about it for sure.

The first thesis for the scientific degree of Technical Diagnostics was prepared in 1962. In my thesis was not an obligatory section about the state of the problem in the USSR and abroad. In this regard, a Special Commission verified, why I have no references to publications of other authors. The Board found that refer to diagnostics impossible, they do not exist. Links to writings on Mathematical Logic and Set Theory I have had.

Tests were built not for the scheme they were for logical formulas. To this end, was developed recording of the scheme as a hierarchical logical formula equivalent the scheme (FES). Each point of the scheme is consistent with a letter or an expression in parentheses. Thus, all constant faults clearly appear in the formula. This allowed the recording of big scheme (even the whole computer) in a hierarchical system of FES. Later it was converted into a hierarchical representation of algorithms (HRA), which significantly advance the writing and debugging of programs. Widely introduce the system in the Soviet Union failed; however, some publications were. I started working in Citibank, but I had no luck. The Administration did not want to put software development dependent on one person. At the same time appeared the object-oriented programming with class libraries and operating system from Microsoft. The latter was more adapted to users; however, it did not give many opportunities of HRA. For example, HRA permits to automate program writing and debugging. In 1990 to Citibank came hard times and along with others, was closed the "Advanced Technology". Probably the only copy of the report is at my home.

I have developed and published in the journal "Automatics and Telemechanic" (1965; the journal was reprinted in English in the United States) an example for which J. P. Roth algorithm (1964) does not work. That is, it is not possible to build a test for a single fault in a simple devise. My algorithm (1958), and program (1962) in theses; allowed to build test for multiple failures.

In 1966, I proved inability to build tests for an arbitrary logical formula (scheme or program) without brute-force. I proposed to design devices adapted for being tested. For some types of schemes, I have proposed algorithms. There were got several patents for devises with testability. Initially, this position was rejected. Even in the 1970's at the International Conference in Leningrad, I was told by a group of American and French scientists in the field of Technical Diagnostics, that they have algorithms for any occasion. If I cannot, then my algorithms are not suitable. I offered an example of a schema for which building test for a single fault required a full loop through all possible input sequences. From this, it appeared that it was not possible to build a more efficient algorithm and the discussion ended. In the thesis for the degree Doctor of Technical Sciences "Synthesis well-testable discrete devices; theory and algorithms" the method have been advanced for circuits with memory.

Doctoral dissertation was prepared in 1971, but scientific councils, to which I have applied, refused to take it under various flimsy pretexts. Finally, in 1978, I managed in the Kiev Institute of Cybernetics of Academy of Sciences of Ukraine. Everyone said to me that I fail. The morning after my defending, the Director of the Institute (academician V. Glushkov) said, "What have you done with my Cyber Centre? It buzzes like disturbed hive. A Kogan from aside received 15:0".

It should be noted that by this time appeared thousands of publications and scientists in the field of Technical Diagnostics. However, the excellent specialists for building tests were long before. Even in the Bible it is written that after creating something new, God is assessed (i.e. diagnosed) it by its all-seeing eye ("and God saw that it was good"). From those distant times, people always tested (diagnosed) things they have created. The more this is done at the repairs. That is, there was no theoretical works, but the practice required to diagnose.

In the United States to continue work in the field of Technical Diagnostics, I failed. It was aware of the view that the establishment of all needed for SDI could be done. There is one problem – the system health management. However, citizenship was required everywhere. Someone told me that I should not so hurry to carry out the KGB job. I replied that he is an idiot and started looking for another job. Earning a pension, I can again do what I like. Nevertheless, during this time, I converted from a specialist in a narrow field to a cheerleader, knowing almost nothing about everything. At 70 years, I retired and start putting memories and ideas.

Ideas were born not today. From 1947, when I listened to College lectures on Physics and Thermodynamics, I disagreed with many of the "generally accepted" provisions. I tried to convince professors that the primary and omnipresent force in nature is gravity. This force leads to ordering. Rather it should be talking not about increasing disorder (Entropy), but about ordering. Professors did not discuss, they sent to many huge books.

These ideas were published on the author's website speculations.us and partially in the books.

To discuss these provisions I failed (from 1947).

Ilya Kogan

52

СИНГУЛЯРНОСТЬ
(ИНТЕРВЬЮ)

Ilya Kogan

СОДЕРЖАНИЕ

Ilya Kogan

1. ПРЕДИСЛОВИЕ

Я очень захотел дать интервью о сингулярности. Но есть проблема, нет желающего меня интервьюировать. А уж очень хочется. И тут я вспомнил, что Киссинджер говорил, что он надеется, что в зале есть люди, которые зададут вопросы для заготовленных им ответов. Именно на эти вопросы он ответит. Ведь вопросов будет заведомо больше, чем можно ответить в выделенное время. То есть, Киссинджер проводил аналогичные интервью.

У меня тоже есть ответы и необходимо написать вопросы. Впрочем, и вопросы тоже есть. Нет журналиста, который выслушает и напечатает интервью в своей статье, но интервью можно издать в брошюре.

Дело за малым, подготовить брошюру с интервью к печати.

Как обычно пишу на русском, чтобы думать только о смысле, а не о подборе слов. Затем перевожу на английский. Этот метод помогает мне и в случае, когда мучает бессонница. Я мысленно перевожу на английский стихи (обычно Пушкина) или песни (обычно Вертинского). В особо тяжелых случаях одеваю наушники и слушаю, гуляя по квартире обходя спальню, чтобы не тревожить сон жены. Слушаю что-то типа "Physics of the Impossible" by Michio Kaku, "The Age of Spiritual Machines", by Ray Kurzweil, или Old Greek Stories. Очень помогает.

Чтобы не выдумывать псевдонимов в работе есть два лица, условно автор раздвоился. Первый интервьюер с именем «Вопрос» или «В.». Второй с именем «Ответ» или «О.».

Вопросы сгруппированы по темам по согласованию с В и О.

При подготовке интервью к печати были внесены некоторые изменения и дополнения. Этот текст выделен шрифтом курсив.

2. ВВЕДЕНИЕ

В.	Уважаемая аудитория, мне выпала честь ведущего в настоящем интервью. На вопросы будет отвечать Доктор Технически наук Илья Коган. Др. Коган является автором более ста научных публикаций, в основном по Технической диагностике. Его публикации на русском языке, но многие были переведены в Соединенных Штатах и переизданы на английском.

Правильно ли я Вас представил?

О.	Да, однако добавлю, Техническая диагностика является наукой близкой к распознаванию образов. Можно утверждать, что она относится к области вычислительных машин и программированию. Впрочем, все это нельзя игнорировать и при анализе явления, называемого сингулярностью.

В моих работах обращается внимание на постановку вопросов, предшествующим математическим построениям, которые возведены над исходными тезисами. В первую очередь это относится к физике. Примером, могут служить работы о квантовом компьютере.

I have heard from very reputable scientists that there are sections where mathematics does not help to find out the crux of the problem. They said that there are cases when it is better to use for proof (in mathematics) reasoning, based on common sense. I would especially like to mention the outstanding mathematicians as I. M. Gelfand, A. Kolmogorov, M. Keldysh and V. Glushkov, from whom I heard such allegations.

Perhaps this was meant by Albert Einstein, expressing the proposal, which is mentioned in Micheo Kaku remarkable book "Physics of the impossible", «Einstein once said that unless a theory can be explained to a child, the theory was probably useless; that is, the essence of a theory has to be captured by a physical picture. So many physicists get lost in a thicket of mathematics that leads nowhere. However, like Newton before him, Einstein was obsessed by the physical picture; the mathematics would come later. For Newton, the physical picture was the falling apple and the moon. Were the forces that made an apple fall identical to the forces that guided the moon in its orbit? When Newton decided that the answer was yes, he created a mathematical architecture for the universe that suddenly unveiled the greatest secret of the heavens, the motion of celestial bodies themselves. »

К сожалению, мне не удалось добиться ни разу обсуждения исходных соображений, которые являются основой наслоений в виде математических построений.

В.	Давно ли Вас интересуют проблемы, связанные с сингулярностью?

О.	Задолго до появления понятия сингулярность в отношении к вычислительным системам. Мне приходилось анализировать это понятие (или эту проблему) в лекциях на тему применения вычислительных машин в научно-исследовательских и конструкторских работах. Популярны были вопросы о том будет ли машина мыслить. В 1950 И. Сталин высказался, что машина никогда не будут переводчиком. Я вызвал дискуссию по этому вопросу в институте. Фактически это было обсуждение вопроса о возможных способностях машин. Еще о том, можно ли ограничивать возможности науки. Дискуссию запретил парторг института; нельзя обсуждать мнение Сталина.

Например, мое сорокалетие (1969) отмечалось в одесской пивной Гамбринус. Мы (сотрудники отдела) сидели на бочонках(стульях); один сотрудник читал свои соображения о будущем нашего отдела. Отдел будет называться «Высре на куримо». Это непереводимое сокращение (звучащее по-русски на грани приличия) от «Вычислительной среды на куриных мозгах» (Вычислительные (ВЫ) среды (СРЕ) на куриных (КУРИ) мо (МОЗГАХ)). Автором за несколько часов были изложены обоснования почему мной были выбраны именно куриные мозги для создания сверх интеллектуальной системы (понятие сингулярность еще не было широко известно). Пример приведен чтобы подчеркнуть, что тема сингулярность для меня не нова. Эта тема мне была интересна задолго до описанного примера. К тому же она была близка к тематике отдела.

Мой путь в диагностику (и в науку) более подробно изложен в приложении.

В.	Определите пожалуйста понятие сингулярность.

О.	Под сингулярностью я понимаю систему, которая имеет IQ не ниже среднего IQ человека. Предполагаю, что эта система может пройти тест Тьюринга. У вычислительной системы, участвовавшей в Jeopardy, не измерялся IQ и, тем не менее можно утверждать, что она прошла тест Тьюринга.

В.	В теме о сингулярности уделяется большое внимание человеческому мозгу.

О.	Это естественно, ведь сингулярность — это программа, и вычислительная машина в которой работает эта программа. В сингулярности можно разделить программное обеспечение и «железо», но в работе они являются одним целым. Я не «открываю Америку», Р. Курцвейл обоснованно утверждает, что человек это скорее software, то есть человеческую личность можно описать и хранить в виде файла. Свое физическое воплощение сингулярность определит самостоятельно.

В.   Что вы скажете о наличии сознания у сингулярности.

О.   Если человек это software, то сознание это некоторая подпрограмма. Если нет, то придется выйти за Законы Сохранения. Там я бессилен. Аналогично можно говорить о сексе, о настроении и так далее.

В.   Может ли существовать общество, в котором на равных правах участвуют одновременно люди и вычислительные машины, то есть сингулярности.

О.   Безусловно. Единственное условие — это близость IQ членов общества. Этот вопрос уже рассматривался в моей книге **SINGULARITY WHERE IS IT? (second edition),** смотри на AMAZON. Первое издание книги в 2007 году.

В.   Название книги говорит, что вы ставите под сомнение близость появления сингулярности.

О.   Именно это я рассмотрел и пытался обосновать в книге.

В.   Вы против понятия сингулярность?

О.   Что Вы! Я уверен в его полезности. Мне очень нравится описание сингулярности в блестящих книгах Р. Курцвейла. Просто я не уверен в близости появления сингулярности. Мой вопрос, где она. Сейчас, апрель 2018 в Конгрессе «судят» Facebook. Оказалось, что «судьи» показали свою полную несостоятельность и непонимание вопросов, связанных с ролью, возможностями и работой вычислительных систем. А ведь это уже настоящее и ближайшее будущее нашего общества, нашей страны.

В.   Не сильно ли Вы строги?

О.   Скорее наоборот.

В.   Определите свой взгляд на действительность, например, религию.

О.   Я не религиозен. Это не только потому, что вырос (до 57 лет) в стране, где религия упоминалась как «опиум для народа». Я давно понял, что многие общественные философии эквивалентны религии, что самой ортодоксальной религией является исторический материализм.

Особенно его практика. Ведь именно коммунисты подняли вопрос о возможности создания социализма с человеческим лицом. Я давно понял, что многие религии являются ортодоксальными политическими партиями.

В основе моего мировоззрения лежит незыблемость ЗАКОНОВ СОХРАНЕНИЯ. Именно из этих законов следует невозможность мгновенных действий. Они не допускают бесконечных скоростей. Они требуют относительности при наблюдении явлений природы. Явления, которым А. Эйнштейн назвал свою теорию. Они не допускают сотворения чего-либо из ничего. То есть Вселенная (пространство, время, энергия) вечна и бесконечна. Из них следуют поведение гироскопа и первый закон Ньютона.

Подчеркну, что это не уменьшает величия ученых их сформулировавших впервые.

Из них следуют утверждения типа:

- Все, что не запрещено, неизбежно сбудется (Anything that is not forbidden is mandatory! T. H. White).

- Эволюция не злонамерена, она неизбежна (А. Эйнштейн).

То есть обязательно появятся и человек, и сингулярность.

3. ПРОБЛЕМЫ СОЗДАНИЯ СИНГУЛЯРНОСТИ

В.   Остановитесь подробнее на Вашем видении сингулярности.

О.   Сингулярность — это мощная система программного обеспечения. Для работы сингулярности требуется мощная вычислительная система.

- Подобная система требует большую память для ее хранения и работы.

- Она требует значительного быстродействия вычислительной машины, на которой программы будут работать.

- Требуется высокая надежность системы.

В.   Вы кажется сказали, что все это уже есть.

О.   Система, которая, по моему мнению, прошла тест Тьюринга была продемонстрирована ее игрой в Jeopardy. Однако, это эксперимент, который продемонстрировал возможность. Я играю в шахматы, но между мной и Каспаровым огромная пропасть. Здесь и годы труда и многое другое.

В.   Расшифруйте что ещё. Как вы сказали «многое другое».

О.   Проблем много.

1. Философские проблемы, как например,

- Место сингулярности в обществе.

- Сосуществование сингулярности и человека.

- Будет ли сингулярность представлена в единичном экземпляре или это будет множество самостоятельных систем (общество).

- Длительность жизни сингулярности.

- Место сингулярности в эволюции природы.

2. Технические проблемы.

- Разработка требований к системе обеспечивающей функционирование сингулярности.

- Создание вычислительной системы, которая обеспечит устойчивое и надежное функционирование сингулярности.

- Связь сингулярности с окружающей средой.

- Возможные технические ограничения и их причины.

3. Математическое обеспечение системы (сингулярности).

- Создание алгоритмов работы сингулярности.

Перечисленные вопросы не изолированные и их решения влияют друг на друга. Каждый пункт требует серьёзного рассмотрения.

В.   Так и поступим, остановимся подробнее на технических проблемах.

О.   Есть высказывания, что вычислительная мощность, которая может быть создана во Вселенной достигает 10^{80} os (operation per second). Теоретический расчёт верен, однако не рассмотрена живучесть этой системы и возможности ее обслуживания. Может оказаться, что вычислительная мощность окажется значительно ниже расчётной и даже ниже требуемой для работы сингулярности.

Вопросы обеспечения надежного функционирования требуют введения дополнительного оборудования, которое понизит быстродействие и увеличит объем системы. Избыточность увеличивает размеры и снижает быстродействие системы. Избыточность вводит в систему структуры, которые принципиально не тестируемы при использовании только рабочих входов системы.

Я понимаю, что «может оказаться» не является доказательством, однако вопрос должен быть рассмотрен.

В.   Какие трудности или противоречия технического характера вы можете назвать.

О.   Приведу лишь несколько примеров,

- Скорость работы. Если верен принцип удвоения мощности за два года (или за сто лет), то за сто миллионов лет скорость работы технической базы возрастет до неимоверных размеров. Величина 10^{80} os покажется мизерной. Впрочем, допущение мгновенного проявления результатов эксперимента допускает бесконечных скоростей.

- Рост скорости требует увеличения плотности элементов, сокращения их размеров, Как следствие повышения чувствительности к внешним полям. То есть падает живучесть Сингулярности.

- Появляется проблема введения избыточности, что может остановить повышение скорости.

Конечно, если допускаются бесконечные скорости, то все проблемы, рассматриваемые в настоящей работе, исчезают. Напомню, что я сторонник Законов Сохранения, а не божественной волшебной палочки. Я допускаю существование очень мощного Бога, но не всемогущего.

В. Перейдем к математическому обеспечению.

О. Сегодня есть лишь предположения о работе подобных систем. Единственным примером является мозг человека. Имеются предположения как мозг организует мышление которые не безупречны.

Например, известно явление обучения. Человеку рассказывают правила некоторой незнакомой ему игры. Выслушав, он сразу начинает играть в эту игру и даже обыгрывает своего учителя. Трудно объяснить это явление на основе нейронных сетей, генетических алгоритмов, или рекурсивных вычислений. Трудно построить требуемый путь эволюции из мелких шагов на этих принципах.

Эксперименты со структурами типа конечных автоматов позволяют утверждать, что этого может добиться эволюция из мелких шагов. Необходимо математическое обеспечение, позволяющее создавать структуру аналогичную конечному автомату и изменять эту структуру в процессе обмена информацией с окружающей средой.

В.   Каковы отличия эволюции сингулярности и живых существ.

О.   Эволюция сингулярности принципиально отличается от эволюции живых существ. Мозг может изменять свою структуру малыми шагами от поколения к поколению. Новое поколение сингулярности может значительно отличаться от предыдущего. Для этого должны быть предусмотрены в математическом и техническом обеспечении соответствующие возможности. Эти возможности разрабатываются известными методами, техническое задание, технический проект. Далее создание опытных образцов и экспериментирование.

В.	Как связаны математическое и техническое обеспечения.

О.	Например, при обеспечении надёжности можно влиять на качество элементной базы. Можно строить надежные структуры из ненадежных элементов. Можно проводить тестирование и ремонт в реальном масштабе времени. Можно проводить повышение живучести путем защищенного кодирования. Можно строить системы надежных вычислений. Примером может служить сравнение результатов повторных вычислений. Все эти методы допускают комбинирование.

В.	Перейдем к философии.

О.	Здесь я боюсь рассуждать. Ведь этим будет заниматься существенно более интеллектуальная система – сингулярность. Если такая система возможна, то есть эволюция уже не создала наиболее мощную интеллектуальную систему – человеческий мозг.

Если сингулярность может иметь интеллект, значительно превышающий интеллект человека, то человеку нет места в обществе сингулярности. Вспомните, «В Планете Обезьян» люди сидят в зоопарке в клетках.

В.	Ваш взгляд на существование сингулярности.

О.	С зарождением вселенной неизбежно появление Сингулярности. На это требуется примерно пять миллиардов лет.

Если вселенная замкнутая, то время жизни сингулярности порядка 10 миллиардов лет. Напомню, что это происходит в условиях действия Закона Ускорения Развития. Подчеркну, что я верю в этот закон. При новом цикле развития все повторится.

Если вселенная не замкнутая, то она будет расширяться бесконечно долго. Соответственно возрастает время жизни и развития сингулярности. Однако принципиальные изменения в развитии сингулярности должны произойти в первые миллиарды лет после ее появления.

Предполагается, что на этом начальном участке существования будут решены все философские вопросы.

Если пространство бесконечно и в нем существуют локальные вселенные. Принципиальных отличий не будет.

Сингулярность не сможет переместиться из одной локальной вселенной в соседнюю. Она будет разрушена излучением Большого Взрыва в соседних вселенных при перемещении в между-вселенском пространстве. Это произойдёт и для открытой локальной вселенной.

Переносу зачатков жизни между вселенными излучение Больших Взрывов не помешает.

В.   Приведенное выше является фантазией, но может иметь и научное обоснование?

О.   Многое приведено в моих книгах (смотри ссылки в «RESULTS 2017» на AMAZON). Иногда в виде полу-фантастики, как результаты профессора Multyrock в ее Теории Абсолютного Пространства.

Тем не менее, описанная Лаборатория Анализа Развития (LAD) может иметь научную базу на основе Теории эволюции. LAD сегодня позволяет приступить к созданию экспериментальной базы на основе трехмерной печати.

Видимо при решении вопросов мышления в живой природе, необходимо выделять участки нервной системы, которые похожи на структуры типа конечных автоматов.

Очевидно, что у человека это будет неокортекс. Какие это участки у дельфинов или осьминогов. Какие это участки у собаки, которая водит машину. Это можно определить без разрушающих экспериментов.

Не все эксперименты сегодня осуществимы. Эксперименты исследования Теории Абсолютного Пространства сегодня недоступны, но принципиально возможны.

Общественно - политические вопросы

В.   Какое будущее у человечества?

О.   Благодаря гению Э. Теллера практически исчезла опасность самоуничтожения человечества. Термоядерное оружие сделало войну бессмысленной. Всякие «правозащитники» (а вернее поджигатели) даже придумали (для Э. Теллера) Шнобелевскую премию (*Ig Nobel Prize*).

Однако, этим они только возвеличили гений Э. Теллера.

Об этом я писал неоднократно. Возможны два вида будущего,

- Смешанное (люди и машины) общество.

- Чисто машинное общество.

В.   Есть ли переходный процесс от сегодня до «светлого» будущего?

О.   Видимо это будет что-то близкое описанному в других моих книгах. На Земле будет единое государство с одним языком. Население порядка одного – двух миллиардов. Население будет жить в домах – городах, окруженных зонами типа Орландо. Основным положением, определяющим жизнь будет «Кодекс Стабильности». В каждом доме будет до миллиона жителей. В каждой квартире стены будут покрыты обоями – телеэкранами. На эти экраны кроме текущих программ можно будет вызывать любое культурное или историческое событие на нужном языке.

Политическая структура близка к США. Группа домов объединена в штаты, которые имеют центральное правительство. Под потолком экран – лента, которая позволяет проводить опросы, референдумы и голосование. Это позволяет быстро определить мнение общества и делает ненужными многолюдные протесты.

В.   Каков вклад стран в цивилизацию.

О.   Я не компетентен, но один случая расскажу. В Соборе Парижской Богоматери экскурсовод долго говорит не о соборе, а о вкладе Франции в демократию. Она обратилась к нам с просьбой сказать свое мнение. Я сказал, что известно, что Франция дала миру гильотину, а Англия Гайд-парк. По ее взгляду я понял, что она сожалеет, что у нее нет гильотины.

В.   А о России?

О.   Россия вполне достойна места во второй десятке развитых стран. Ведь в мире, есть США, Китай, Франция, Англия и так далее. Каждый политик России, который пророчит ей ведущее, заведомо первое, место в мире объективно злейший враг России. Каждый политик, который постоянно не сравнивает Россию с Норвегией – враг России.

В.   Что мешает развитию цивилизации?

О   Политкорректность. Трудно найти более вредное для общества течение. Даже внедрение спорта в среде выходцев из Африки меньше влияет на общество. Это просто скрытый расизм.

В.   Можно ли справиться с огромным разрывом в уровне развитых и бедных стран в мире; с разрывом между разными слоями населения внутри стран?

О.   Сегодня технологически вполне возможно производить достаточно продуктов питания и основных продуктов жизнеобеспечения, которые будут доступны (практически бесплатно) всему населению Земли.

Более существенные трудности в уничтожении психологического барьера. Например, «Почему Трампу, Гейтсу доступно, а мне нет». Как уничтожить животную зависть сытого, одетого человека, живущего в удобной квартире, к более богатым – не знаю, однако уверен, что это возможно.

ЭПИЛОГ

В.   Ваше видение будущего.

О.   Не знаю, однако …

Как я уже писал человечество достигнет всеобщего благосостояния. Это ближе, чем близкая сингулярность. Все обеспечены едой, квартирой, зрелищами. Все делают автоматы. Нет болезней.

Однако желание и зависть неустранимы. Например, миллион хочет самый роскошный дворец на вершине Эльбруса. Конечно всем все по потребностям, но вершина одна. Кто решит кому ее отдать. Видимо без инструктора Райкома при коммунизме не обойтись.

И вот появилась сингулярность. Здесь заведомо каждому по потребностям. Какие у нее потребности? С. Лем не написал, чем живет сингулярность, его океан на Солярисе.

Видимо об это можно писать только для современного человечества. Я пытался к этому обратиться в брошюре, которую так и назвал
«ВСЕ НЕ ТАК КАК ЕСТЬ».

Заключение

В.   Позвольте мне поблагодарить Доктора Когана за его работу.

О.   Хочу поблагодарить аудиторию за проявленное терпение.

4. ЖИЗНЬ (ПРИЛОЖЕНИЕ)

Примите эту главу как пособие для профессоров и юристов «свободного мира». Используя ново-речь Большого Брата они себя назвали демократами.

Клинтоны или сандерсы хорошо знают за какие блага, богатства и власть они борются.

4.1. Все просто

Когда думаю о жизни, то первое, что вспоминаю как мама вернулась из военкомата (1945), где ей вручили документ о смерти Давида.

Вдруг я услышал страшный стон, вопль, вой. Она запела «Напрасно старушка ждет сына домой, ей скажут она зарыдает …». Она занесла над головой топор, который я успел отвести. Да, в 50 она вдруг стала старушкой. Старой, старой, она сгорбилась и осунулась за несколько минут. Эта сцена и страшный отзвук периодически посещают меня. Видимо это будет моим последним видением в жизни.

Для каждой матери ее сын бесконечно дорог. Командующий может послать миллионы таких в огонь Ржева или в воды Волги. Авось один из ста достигнет (то есть его плот доплывет) Сталинграда. Потом он спокойно скажет, «Бабы новых нарожают.» (как Жуков).

Я оглянулся и обнаружил огромную пропасть между моим детством и сегодня. По этой причине кратко описана моя жизнь и выделены особо важные положения. Читателя могут удивить даты. В США многое было на десятилетия раньше. Однако производство современного вооружения в СССР не уступало по качеству и значительно превосходило по количеству. Это не интересует социалистов, которые в США называются демократами. Они вспомнят песни Галича, когда окажутся в ГУЛАГе, созданной ими страны. Не дай Бог!

Напомню несколько эпизодов из жизни, которые могли существенно на нее повлиять.

1941, я пошел за продуктами, вернулся, а наш эшелон ушел. Сел на тот о котором сказали, что он идет в нужную сторону. Платформы со стаканами для снарядов. Подходит группа ребят. Сначала съедают все, что я купил. Затем играют в карты и двое, выигравших заявляют, что они возьмут меня за руки и за ноги и раскачав сбросят. Я открыл перочинный ножик, взял во вторую руку снаряд и сказал, подходите. Вожаку это понравилось Он был заметно крупнее остальных.

Он сказал, что я могу отыграться, что я и сделал. Шайка ехала в Узбекистан на зимовку, там они «попадались» и их определяли в детдом. Весной они обкрадывали детдом и ехали воровать в Сибирь. В Узбекистане воровать было опасно. Узбеки забивали сапогами воришку до смерти.

Мне не пришлось участвовать в их делах, я играл на пару с вожаком. Мы всех обчищали и меня ненавидели.

Когда продавали весной краденое, я на базаре увидел маму. Проследил и зашел к ней. Она что-то продала из вещей и вечером уезжала из Маргилана в село под Андижаном, где жил (нашелся через Бугуруслан) средний брат. Он отстал от эшелона на три недели раньше меня. Я объяснил ей ситуацию и сказал, что обязательно приеду.

Вечером на станции Горчаково была облава. Нашего вожака схватили как дезертира. Все разбежались, и я нашел маму в ее поезде.

Брата вскоре призвали в армию. Мы переехали под Фергану, где жила жена маминого брата. Оказалось, что в школу я ходить не могу, по дороге меня избивают, как порхатого жиденка. Я не мог идти в класс с лицом, залитым кровью. Пошел учеником фрезеровщика на текстильный комбинат. Смены, неделя с 7 утра до 7 вечера, следом с 7 вечера до 7 утра. Без выходных и 30 мин перерыв.

1944, освободили Николаев, и мы вернулись. Поступил на завод фрезеровщиком. Затем в ремесленное училище на модельщика по дереву и в вечернюю школу. Брат погиб 21 января 1945 года и в последнем письме просил меня учиться.

1947, сдал экзамены на аттестат зрелости, и по результатам должен получить золотую медаль. Мне выдали все документы, как медалисту, кроме аттестата. В институтах кончаются вступительные экзамены, а я не могу подать документы. Меня вызывает директор и предлагает выбрать по каким предметам мне поставят четверки и дадут простой аттестат. Приезжаю в Институт Связи и меня принимают без экзаменов.

1950, кончаю третий курс и у мамы кровоизлияние, парализована левая сторона тела. Сначала она в больнице, а потом дома.

Я утром хожу в больницу, а оттуда в яхт-клуб. Питаюсь черствым хлебом с водой. Мне дают лодку на студенческой станции. Замечаю на берегу знакомого и подъезжаю чтобы позвать в лодку. Он говорит, что познакомит меня с девочками. Я знакомлюсь и одна с очаровательной улыбкой соглашается поехать со мной. Вот мы с тех пор неразлучны примерно 70 лет.

Договариваюсь с женщиной, которая будет у нас жить и помогать маме. В октябре получаю телеграмму, срочно приезжай, мама одна. Двери открыты, забегаю в квартиру и слышу истошный крик, скорее подсов. Иду выливать подсов в туалет, который в конце двора. Возвращаюсь и обнаруживаю, что в нетопленой квартире, кроме кровати, в которой мама, поломанной табуретки и стола нет ничего. Нет ни одной тряпочки или бумажки, горы мусора на полу. Квартира - это две полуподвальные комнаты, без электрического освещения, ближайшая вода во дворе за углом. В продуктовых магазинах пустые полки (1950), но и денег нет.

Наладил жизнь, встаю до рассвета, чищу и затапливаю плиту, кормлю маму и сажусь за учебники. Вечером иду к Миле. Через полвека понял, что это было мое спасение, я не думал о будущем. Бесконечные, темные, зимние вечера; какие страшные мысли могли родиться в моей голове.

1951, обнаруживается, что я уже месяцы не был на лекциях. Я приезжал на день, сдавал все экзамены, лабораторные, контрольные, зачеты и так далее. Ходят слухи, что больная мама — это моя выдумка, что я в Николаеве я из-за девочки.

Меня вызывают на заседание бюро комсомольской организации. Ставится вопрос о моем исключении, как следствие армия.

Мой друг говорит секретарю Паркома института Паншину (он был председателем приемной комиссии и способствовал моему поступлению в институт), который присутствует, что нужен перерыв. Он рассказывает правду, и Паншин спрашивает меня, ведь через два месяца практика в Кишиневе. Я выдумываю, что врачи сказали, что через месяц мама поднимется.

Мне начинают предлагать помощь. Показываю зачетку, в которой все пятерки и говорю, что сам справлюсь. Одна девочка говорит, что поедет в Николаев помочь. Я взорвался и заорал, ты будешь подавать маме подсов и спать со мной на столе. … Тишина и заседание закрыли.

Через месяц я очередной раз приезжаю в Одессу, а там меня ждет телеграмма о смерти мамы. Похороны, я оставил открытую квартиру и прямо с кладбища уехал в Одессу. Началась нормальная студенческая жизнь.

В аспирантуре меня не оставили, но назначение было очень удачным. В Ереване строили подземную радиостанцию, где я работал монтажником и наладчиком с лучшими специалистами страны.

1953, приезжаю в Николаев за Милой, мы расписались.

Впрочем, ее «друзья» меня предупредили.

- Ты прожил тяжелую жизнь. Правды никто не знал. Ни одного человека я не приводил домой, никому не рассказывал о своей жизни в то время.

- Она избалованная кошечка, в институте ее называют аристократкой.

- Вы не найдете общего языка, подумай.

Молодость безрассудна. Через пять дней я слушаю ее концерты в ущелье у речки. Мила работала со мной и пела мне в ближайшем ущелье. У нее очень сильное колоратурное сопрано. Голос разносился далеко в горах, а я запомнил все партии опер и оперетт.

Прошло много лет, и мы все это время неразлучны. Кажется, что все больше тяготеем друг к другу. Конечно время влияет. У меня неизменный вес, но лысина. Кажется, я сейчас менее твердо стою на полу на двух ногах, чем тогда на одной руке на перилах балкона. И память стала странной. Я помню расположение всех 18 кроватей в общежитии и всех, кто где спал (1947), я помню их имена. В 1934 я повторял за ребе заупокойную молитву, и он мне рассказывал эпизоды еврейской истории. Я помню эти беседы. Я помню таблицы интегралов. Однако, я не помню, о чем говорил несколько минут назад. Мила сохранила подвижность и прочее.

1956, тесть зовет в Николаев. 16 апреля отменили крепостное право, мы подали заявления и уехали. Но в Николаеве нам работы нет, нет ее и других 63 городах, куда я написал. Работал временно плотником. Поехал в Москву и в министерствах подходил к каждому солидному мужчине. Так наткнулся на заместителя директора Кироваканского «НИИАвтоматика».

Приготовились ехать, но меня призвали на четыре месяца на курсы переподготовки офицеров. За это время прибыл отказ из Кировакана. Тесть пошел со мной к второму секретарю Обкома, и он устроил меня сменным инженером на радиоцентр. Через месяц меня уволили. Я искал на грунтовой дороге каменистый участок, чтобы покончить с собой.

Посовещались и решили, что я поеду в Кировакан и скажу, что был в лагерях и письмо не получал. Приехал, меня сразу оформили и дали прекрасную квартиру. Письмо было не от руководства.

Работа навела меня на золотую жилу «техническую диагностику».

1986, мы в США и с 70 на пенсии.

4.2. С другой стороны

Я, Коган Илья Вениаминович, *еврей по национальности*, родился 5 сентября 1929 года в городе Вознесенске. Структура первой фразы была дана, как обязательная, полковником, членом КПСС, начальником Ворошиловского райвоенкомата Одессы. В 1952 году, мы, в военкомате, писали свои автобиографии для присуждение офицерского звания. Слова в италик были удалены по указанию Начальника Котайкского райвоенкомата Армении в 1953 году. Одесскую биографию он дал мне, сказав, что это документ, заверенный подписью и печатью Ворошиловского военкомата и может мне пригодиться.

В 1932 году наводнение разрушило город Вознесенск и наш дом. Мы переехали в г. Николаев, где сняли полуподвальную кухню. Большую ее часть занимала огромная русская печь. Печь требовала много топлива и зимой было холодно. Электричества (у нас), канализации, и водопровода на было. В моем окружении было много таких как я. Нам не хватало всего, но мы не голодали. Отмечу, что даже голодомор не касался городов. Им члены КПСС задушили сельское население, которому доступ в города был закрыт армией.

1934, я и другие дети выбегали, на улицу. Хлопали и пели если пролетает самолет или проезжает автомобиль. Семейные фотографии можно пересчитать по пальцам одной руки.

Были в моей жизни и светлые стороны. Во дворе жили: Дина Яковлевна Заславская, дети которой жили в США. Историк Владимир Вячеславович с женой – тетей Дусей. Инженер Антон Яковлевич Карно с женой - врачом Софией Соломоновной. Я был на всех один ребенок.

В Николаеве жила мамина сестра с мужем, у них тоже не было детей. Ее муж - дядя Сережа задаривал меня великолепными конструкторами и разными наборами инструментов. Еще он дарил прекрасные книги и выписывал мне газеты и разные издания типа «Для умелых рук».

Ilya Kogan

1937, А. Я. купил радиоприемник и фотоаппарат. В ворота военной части, которые рядом, въезжают танки и пушки. Нам поставили (бесплатно) радиоточку. По углам на столбах поставили громкоговорители.

Была неприятная обязанность, обойти улицы и собрать лошадиный и коровий навоз. Из него с угольной крошкой лепили лепешки, которыми топили зимой.

И все же, мне было лучше, чем многим моим сверстникам. Сад, весной утопающий в разноцветной сирени и других цветущих кустах, и деревьях. Три огромных шелковичных дерева кормивших нас два месяца. И вяз с расходящимися тремя стволами, с ветками гибкими как веревки, с огромной густой кроной.

Там были наши шалаши, индейские наряды и луки. Там я привязывал хитроумными узлами моего 10-летнего брата, завешивал окна и закрывал двери. Я делал шахматный ход и выходил сказать ему. Но в первую очередь проверял, как он привязан. Я проигрывал и недоумевал, как ему удается так быстро развязаться, подсмотреть позицию и снова залезть, и привязаться. Что можно играть «в слепую» я не верил.

Брата я обожал, он был лучший драчун, чемпион города среди подростков по шахматам и по плаванию. Поступая в школу, я уже выучил вместе с братом программу первых четырех классов.

1939, хлеб по карточкам.

В 1941 началась война; мы эвакуировались. Сначала брат, а потом я отстал от эшелона и шатался с какой-то шайкой воришек. Жил в детском доме. Маму встретил в Маргилане в 1942. Переехали с ней к брату в село около Андижана. Его вскоре призвали в армию.

Мы переехали в текстильный городок под Ферганой. Жили в комнате, где еще жили, пожилая женщина и мама с дочкой. Они пережили блокаду и только двое, из большой семьи, выжили. От них я знаю подробности блокадного Ленинграда.

В школу я не мог ходить. На улице меня ожидали мальчишки, которым доставляло удовольствие избить «жиденка». Если я пытался отбиться. То меня хватали за руки и били пока лицо не было залито кровью. Я прибегал домой и плакал, скорее не от боли, а от несправедливой обиды.

Пошел работать учеником фрезеровщика. Работа была без выходных; неделя с 7 утра до 7 вечера, неделя с 7 вечера до 7 утра, 30 мин перерыв на еду, которой практически не было. В то время я мечтал и днём и во сне только о еде (любой еде). Ноги пухли от голода и через день жестокий приступ малярии.

1943, мой новый фрезерный станок имеет свой электромотор. Все остальные станки движутся от шкивов на оси под потолком.

В 1944, вернулись в Николаев. Поступил на завод, но туда без обуви не пускали, а в колодках ходить я стеснялся. В школу ходил босым. Брат написал, чтобы я пошел в школу, но вместо его офицерского аттестата пришли свидетельство о смерти и ордена. Пошел в ремесленное училище и в вечернюю школу. Пошел по возрасту в восьмой класс (в 5, 6, и 7 я не учился).

По окончании школы (1947) пытались сорвать мое поступление в институт. По итогам мне полагалась золотая медаль, но выдали простой аттестат с задержкой. Уже было поздно сдавать вступительные экзамены, но (о чудо!) меня приняли.

И вот я в студенческом общежитии. Я сплю на простынях, как и другие 17 моих соседей по комнате. Впервые в жизни, уютно, весело дружественно.

Трудно, нужно работать и помогать маме. И вдруг у нее инсульт. Она не может быть одна парализованная в холодном и темном подвале. Я ухаживаю за ней в Николаеве и «учусь» в Одессе. Второй инсульт и я один.

Однако, я наконец почувствовал все прелести студенческой жизни.

1950, участвую в создании любительского телецентра. В нашей комнате у одного студента (из 18) есть фотоаппарат.

1952, монтажник и наладчик мощного подземного радиоцентра. Кроме генераторов с лампами с мой рост, есть много интересного. Например, регенераторы атмосферы и герметическая защита. У меня свой фотоаппарат.

В 1956 тесть убедил нас переехать к ним в Николаев. Оказалось, что там мне, кроме временных работ типа плотника, везде отказывали. Я был высококвалифицированным специалистом по монтажу и настройке радиотехнической аппаратуры. Это была одна из наиболее востребованных специальностей в СССР в то время. Однако такова была политика членов КПСС. Я написал в 63 областных центра, но везде отказы. Вернулись в Армению.

1957, моделирую системы управления на аналоговых машинах. Программирую на цифровых машинах (1960).

Меня три раза приглашали к себе в аспирантуру известные профессора. По разным формальным причинам меня не допускали к вступительным экзаменам.

Сейчас в США (2016) прошла избирательная компания. Профессора и студенты хотят затянуть страну в социализм. Трудно не верить лжи социалистов. Черчилль отметил, что тот, кто не верит в социализм в 18 не имеет сердца, но если верит в 30, то у него нет ума.

1987, моделирую нейронные сети и генетические алгоритмы в США. Появляется интернет.

Это моя жизнь, но это и действительность, созданная членами КПСС. Это то, к чему призывают профессора и студенты. Видимо «они не ведают что творят». Если, не дай бог победят, то они первыми будут замучены в ГУЛАГе ими созданном.

Я прожил там 57 лет и мне пришлось встречаться и иметь длительные беседы с очень ответственными людьми. Я изучал потоки информации в Типовом Звене Общегосударственной Автоматизированной

Системы Управления. Я был научным руководителем этой темы.

Моя первая наемная работа была в 1942, помощник электромонтёра. Фактически я работал с раннего детства. Это уборка, чистка плиты, топка и так далее.

После института направили на строительство мощного подземного радиотехнического объекта в горах Армении.

Как соискатель (то есть без научных руководителей) защитил кандидатскую и докторскую диссертации. На утро после защиты докторской академик Глушков сказал: Что вы сделали с моим Кибернетическим центром. Он гудит как растревоженный улей. Чужой Коган получил 15:0.

Жили и работали в Ереване, Кировакане, Николаеве, Одессе и Риге.

В 1986 году переехали в Нью-Йорк, США. В США работали с женой до 70, и вот мы пенсионеры. Живем на третьем этаже своего дома. Ниже дети и внуки, которым нет времени к нам заглядывать они говорят со мной только по-русски, английский, забывается.

Живем вдвоем (женился в 1953), друзья и знакомые «уходят». Те что остались не водят машины и не ходят по лестницам; говорим по телефону и изредка их навещаем. Мы стараемся быть подвижными и пока это удаётся; лифты-кресла на лестницах пока не требуются.

2000, пенсионер, дома много компьютеров, фото камер, машина, холодильник, телевизоры, радо-телефоны. Автомат поддерживает температуру. На улице у прохожих телефоны – компьютеры. Редко происходит важное событие, которое кто-то не заснял на видео.

Много ездили, например, в Европе были более 10 раз. Были в Японии, Сингапуре, Аргентине, Бразилии и так далее.

Увлекался гимнастикой и греблей. В 1952 на Всесоюзных соревнованиях был вторым. Зрители на берегу утверждали, что наша байдарка первой пересекла финиш. Мне (по секрету) сказали, что судьи не могли дать первенство беспартийному еврею. Ведь чемпиону через месяц ехать на первенство мира, за границу. Говорили, что вторые стали там чемпионами.

Перечислю мои квалификации, только те, которые были подтверждены официально.

1942, монтер телефонных сетей (4-й разряд).

1943, фрезеровщик (5-й разряд).

1944, слесарь инструментальщик (6-й разряд).

1945, формовщик (4-й разряд).

1945, литейщик (4-й разряд).

1945, плотник (4-й разряд).

1946, столяр краснодеревец (5-й разряд).

1947, модельщик по дереву (6-й разряд).

1952, Инженер радиотехник (Диплом с Отличием).

1964, защитил диссертацию на соискание ученой степени Кандидат Технических наук. Москва, Институт Автоматики АН СССР (результат голосования, 16 за и 1 против).

1978, защитил диссертацию на соискание ученой степени Доктор технических наук. Киев, Институт Кибернетики АН УССР (результат голосования 15 за, 0 против).

Как все изменилось за мою жизнь.

НЕМНОГО ПОЛИТИКИ

Рос я обычным советским мальчиком. Талантливые «инженеры человеческих душ» михалковы и маршаки внедрили все в мою голову. Я рос убежденным атеистом. Я был убежден, что буржуи хотят отнять мое «счастливое детство». Верил, что религия – опиум для народа. Не подозревал, что самая ортодоксальная религия –

это проповеди членов КПСС. Что многие религии являются политическими партиями.

1933 Наши злейшие враги – капиталисты. Нет ужаснее Колчака, Деникина и им подобных. Ленин защищал короля только когда играл в шахматы.

Одновременно, я повторял за ребе заупокойную молитву о папе и много говорил с ребе. Дядя Володя обсуждал со мной историю от Древнего Египта до наших дней. Особенно много он говорил о возникновении религий и «врагах народа» типа Троцкого. Женщины, которых я по вечерам спасал от комаров дымом, напоминали, что я должен хорошо учиться. Иначе не попаду в процентную норму.

В 1936 году на огромной площади «61 коммунара», был открытый суд при огромном стечении народа. Судили банду «спекулянтов и кровопивцев». Видимо случайно там были только евреи. Однако в толпе открыто говорили, что наконец жидам дали прикурить. Членом этой банды была мамина старшая сестра Хава. Она жила с дочкой и сыном в тесной темной коморке, где кроме тряпья, кровати, тумбочки и табуретки ничего не было. Позднее я узнал, что такие процессы проходили и в других городах. То есть это была целенаправленная акция членов КПСС в масштабах страны.

О происхождении названия площади говорила мемориальная доска, в которой говорилось об этих коммунарах, расстрелянных на площади. Дядя Володя говорил, что это были бандиты и воры, пойманные во время облав на базарах. Их вылавливали и расстреливали не в один день и в разных местах.

1939 фашистская германия и ее лидеры, друзья и враги одновременно. У многих ребят на кисти наколота свастика.

Не знаю какой инстинкт меня предостерег от вопросов воспитательницам в детском саду и потом учителям в школе. Впервые, в 1939 году А. Я., посмотрев, как я рассматриваю гору старых книг и негативов (фото всех «врагов народа»), сказал, чтобы я об этом никому не рассказывал. Иначе дядю Володю и его арестуют. А Вас за что, спросил я, ведь это барахло с его чердака. За то, что я не донес, был ответ. С А. Я. я фотографировал, проявлял и печатал фото. С ним обсуждал фантастические машины, которые собирал из конструкторов, подаренных дядей Сережей.

Я не понимал, что говорю одно, думаю другое, а делаю третье. Через годы я заметил, что так поступает большинство. Видимо, у гомо советикус это врожденное (рефлекс) с давних времен. Иначе зачем искали Рюрика.

2000, о Колчаке, Деникине и других ставят фильмы их с почетом перезахоронили в России.

Мне не раз задавали вопрос, имею ли я, гражданин США, право обсуждать проблемы России. Не буду останавливаться на проблеме свободы высказываний.

Я работал в России более 40 лет (для пенсии необходимо 25). Мои рационализаторские предложения и научные работы дали многомиллионный экономический эффект. Оба моих старших брата были офицерами и погибли на фронте. У мамы было два брата. Моисей, полный кавалер Георгиевского креста, погиб на фронте в 1943. Виктор, командовал артиллерией Сталинграда (согласно мемуарам) и на пенсию вышел Первым Заместителем Командующего Киевского военного округа. Меня выживали патриоты – антисемиты.

Не им решать кому говорить о России. Однако, они снова решают.

МОЙ ПУТЬ В ДИАГНОСТИКУ

В 1952, в п/я 1 города Еревана я впервые столкнулся с тестированием логических устройств. Безопасность и порядок включения оборудования обеспечивали сложные релейные схемы. Они содержали сотни реле с открытыми контактами, которые отказывали. Найти неисправный контакт предполагалось визуально. Я построил для этого системы тестов.

В 1959 году институт получил цифровую машину. Машина заработала, но моя первая программа не идет. В сопровождающей машину документации было написано: «Завод изготовитель гарантирует исправную работу машины при правильном прохождении тестов». Но одна операция сдвига выполнялась неправильно, хоть она проверялась в тесте одиннадцатью операциями. Анализ показал, что достаточно двух операций и тест будет хорошо проверять сдвиг.

Затем я разработал полную теорию построения тестов, которую раскритиковал автор первой книги по решению задач на АЦВМ – Тер Микаелян. Однако, он рекомендовал меня А. А. Ляпунову в Институте Прикладной Математики АН СССР.

В 1962 году на Международном симпозиуме в Москве мой доклад «Контроль Работы Логических Устройств» слушал на английском (в синхронном переводе) профессор Дж. П. Рот, который в 1964 году предложил алгоритм построения тестовых наборов (D – кубы). Труды симпозиума с моим докладом были изданы в США на английском языке. Трудно представить, что Дж. П. Рот не имел у себя книгу с трудами симпозиума. Наши доклады были в одном томе. Это было до подачи его первой работы по диагностике в печать, но ссылки на мою работу он не сделал. Доклад Дж. П. Рота на симпозиуме был не по диагностике («Прагматическая Теория Алгоритмов»). Мою первую печатную работу (1958) он вряд ли видел, но знал о ней заведомо.

Первая диссертация на соискание ученой степени по технической диагностике была подготовлена мной в 1962 году. В моей диссертации не было обязательного раздела о состоянии проблемы в СССР и за рубежом. В этой связи специальная комиссия проверяла, почему у меня нет ссылок на публикации других авторов. Комиссия обнаружила, что ссылаться по диагностике не на кого, а ссылки на труды по математической логике и теории множеств у меня были.

Тесты строились не для схемы, а для логической формулы. С этой целью была разработана запись схемы в виде иерархической логической формулы эквивалентной схеме (ФЭС). Каждой точке схемы соответствовала буква или выражение в скобках. Таким образом, все константные неисправности однозначно отображались в формуле. Это позволяло записывать большие схемы (даже весь компьютер) в виде иерархической системы ФЭС. В дальнейшем это было развито в иерархическую запись алгоритмов (ИЗА), что позволило значительно ускорить написание и отладку программ. Широко внедрить в Советском Союзе мне эту систему не удалось. Я занялся этим, работая в Ситибанке, но и здесь мне не повезло. Администрация не хотела ставить разработку программного обеспечения в зависимость от одного человека. Одновременно появилось объектно-ориентированное программирование с библиотеками классов и операционная система Майкрософт. Последнее было более приспособлено к пользователям, однако, это не давало многих возможностей ИЗА. Например, ИЗА позволяло автоматизировать написание и отладку программ. В 1990 году для Ситибанка наступили тяжелые времена и вместе с другими, был сокращен наш отдел "Advanced Technology". Наверное, единственный экземпляр отчетов по этим работам остался у меня дома.

Мною был приведен и опубликован в журнале «Автоматика и Телемеханика» (1965 год;

журнал переиздавался на английском языке в США) пример, для которого не работал алгоритм (1964) Дж. П. Рота. То есть он не позволял построить тест на одиночную неисправность в простой схеме. Мой алгоритм (и программа, 1958 и 1962) из диссертации позволял построить тест на кратные неисправности.

В 1966 году мною была впервые доказана невозможность построения тестов для произвольной логической формулы (схемы или программы) без полного перебора и предложено проектировать тестируемые устройства. Для некоторых типов схем мною были предложены алгоритмы. Первоначально это положение было отвергнуто. Даже в 1970-х на международной конференции в Ленинграде мне было заявлено группой американских и французских ученых в области технической диагностики, что у них есть алгоритмы на любой случай. Если я не могу, значит, мои алгоритмы не годятся. Мною был предложен пример схемы, для которой построение одного набора теста требовало полного перебора всех возможных входных последовательностей. Из этого следовало, что невозможно построить более эффективный алгоритм и дискуссия завершилась. В диссертации на соискание ученой степени доктора технических наук «Синтез эффективно контролируемых дискретных устройств» теория и алгоритмы были развиты для схем с памятью.

Диссертация была подготовлена в 1971 году, но ученые советы, в которые я обращался, отказывались принять ее к защите под разными надуманными предлогами. Наконец, в 1978 году это мне удалось в киевском Институте Кибернетики АН УССР. Мне все говорили, что это бесполезная затея – провалят. На следующее утро после моей защиты директор института (академик Глушков) сказал: «Что вы сделали с моим Кибернетическим центром? Он гудит как растревоженный улей. Чужой Коган получил 15:0.».

Следует отметить, что к этому времени появились тысячи публикаций и ученых в области технической диагностики. Впрочем, прекрасные специалисты по построению тестов были задолго до меня. Еще в Библии написано, что, создавая что-то новое, Бог оценивал (то есть диагностировал) это своим всевидящим оком («и увидел Бог, что это хорошо»). С тех далеких времен люди всегда проверяли (диагностировали) то, что ими создано. Тем более это делали при ремонтах. То есть не было теоретических работ, но практика требовала диагностировать.

В США продолжить работу в области технической диагностики мне не удалось. Мне было известно мнение, что при создании ПРО все удастся сделать. Есть одна проблема –

работоспособность системы управления. Но везде требовалось гражданство. Кто-то мне прямо сказал, что не следует так торопиться выполнять задание КГБ. Я ответил, что он идиот и начал искать другую работу. Заработав пенсию, я могу снова заниматься, чем нравится, но за это время я из специалиста в узкой области стал дилетантом, почти ничего не знающим обо всем. С 70 лет я на пенсии и излагаю свои воспоминания и идеи.

Идеи родились не сегодня. С 1947 года, когда я в колледже слушал лекции по физике и термодинамике, я не соглашался с многими «общепринятыми» положениями. Я пытался убедить профессоров, что основная и вездесущая сила в природе тяготение. И эта сила ведет к упорядочению. Скорее следует говорить не о возрастании неупорядоченности (энтропии), а об ее убывании. Профессора не дискутировали, они отсылали к множеству огромных книг. Идеи были опубликованы на Интернет-сайте автора speculations.us и, по частям в книгах.

Обсудить эти положения не удалось (с 1947 года).